THE BIKE RACE

BY RACHEL BACH

AMICUS READERS 1 AMICUS INK

amicus readers

Say Hello to Amicus Readers.

You'll find our helpful dog, Amicus, chasing a ball—to let you know the reading level of a book.

1

Learn to Read

High frequency words and close photo-text matches introduce familiar topics and provide ample support for brand new readers.

2

Read Independently

Some repetition is mixed with varied sentence structures and a select amount of new vocabulary words are introduced with text and photo support.

3

Read to Know More

Interesting facts and engaging art and photos give fluent readers fun books both for reading practice and to learn about new topics.

Amicus Readers and Amicus Ink are imprints of Amicus
P.O. Box 1329, Mankato, MN 56002
www.amicuspublishing.us

Library of Congress Cataloging-in-Publication Data
Names: Bach, Rachel, author.
Title: The bike race / by Rachel Bach.
Description: Mankato, Minnesota : Amicus, [2017] | Series: Let's Race
Identifiers: LCCN 2015041503 (print) | LCCN 2015047706 (ebook) | ISBN 9781607539100 (library binding) | ISBN 9781681510347 (eBook) | ISBN 9781681521299 (paperback)
Subjects: LCSH: Bicycle motocross--Juvenile literature. | Extreme sports--Juvenile literature.
Classification: LCC GV1049.3 .B36 2017 (print) | LCC GV1049.3 (ebook) | DDC 796.6/22--dc23
LC record available at http://lccn.loc.gov/2015041503

Editor: Wendy Dieker
Designer: Tracy Myers
Photo Researcher: Derek Brown

Photo Credits: Sergei Bachlakov / Shutterstock.com cover; homydesign / Shutterstock.com 3, 4, 6-7, 8, 10-11, 12-13, 15; dd72 / iStock 16

Printed in the United States of America.

HC 10 9 8 7 6 5 4 3 2 1
PB 10 9 8 7 6 5 4 3 2 1

Today is the bike race!

The riders line up.
Ready, set, go!

Juan is fast.

He goes down first.

Peter is next.

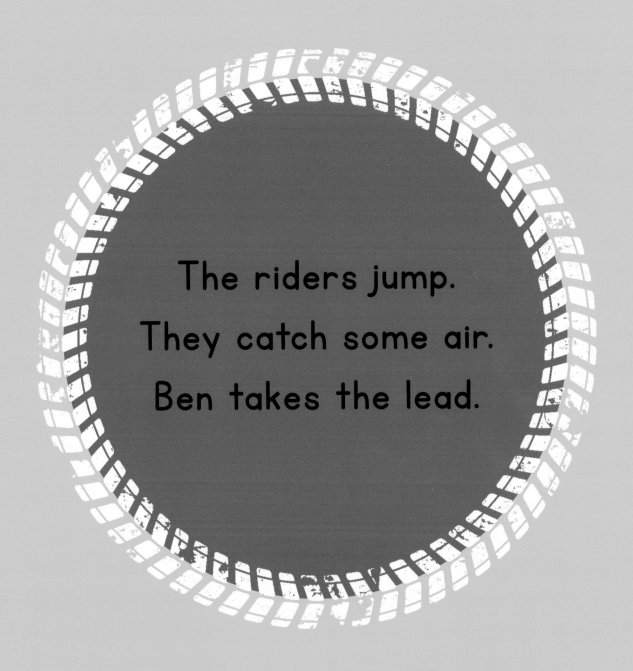

The riders jump.
They catch some air.
Ben takes the lead.

Sam pedals hard.

Now he is in front.

The boys are on
the last lap.
Who will win?

Sam wins!

PARTS OF A BMX BIKE

frame

handlebars

pedals

tire